D1292277

THE SECRET
TO A GREAT GOLF SWING

By Mike Cortson
Past PGA Tour
Player/Manager
The Mike Cortson Company
SHSSH! LLC
© 2006

State Library of Ohio
SEO Library Center
40780 Marietta Road * Caldwell, OH 43724

This book is dedicated to my mother Shirley.

FORE! WORD

"I'm an 18 handicap (actually a 20, but 18 sounds so much better), and that's as good as I'm going to be. So, unless a miracle comes rolling down the fairway, I'm just going to have to be satisfied, breaking 100." How many of us have made that same statement? After lesson, after lesson, after lesson - after video, after video, after video, after golf magazine, after golf magazine, after golf magazine - after nearly giving up the search for the perfect swing - IT HAPPENED, IT REALLY HAPPENED - "THE MIRACLE."

Now we have a golf book for us, for the regular guys and gals. Yes,even for the 18 (?) handicappers. It's all right here, just waiting for you. "THE SECRET - To A Great Golf Swing" is all of that and more. This is the one you have been waiting for. GO TEE IT UP, YOU'RE IN FOR A GREAT BIG SURPRISE."

By: Charlie Jones, famed sportscaster and author, "Be The Ball - The Golf Book For The Mind"

"The Secret"

Introduction

My name is Mike Cortson. I have been a PGA Tour Player Manager for Bruce Crampton for several years. My own skill as a golfer is less than perfect as I have had the misfortune of severe illness visit me. Nevertheless, I have been around the game and golf pros for more years than I care to admit. I have seen more successful golf swings than you can shake a stick at. Some are great to look at and some are just down right unbelievable. I was trained as a lawyer and my eye for detail is quite keen. It is far more difficult to catch a good liar than to catch a great golf swing.

When I took up the game any hope I might have had for turning professional was long past. As most wannabe golfers I decided one day to take up the game. I did the usual and went to the sporting goods store and bought myself all of the latest paraphernalia, loaded up my trunk, drove to the nearest driving range, plopped down a few dollars, took a bucket of balls up to the range, dumped them out onto the ground and began to immediately make a damned fool out of myself. At first I was quite embarrassed. Then I noticed that in the grand scheme of the company I was keeping, I fit right in. I spoke to a few guys and they offered me all sorts of advice. You'd think I was at a surgeon's convention and had a cancerous mole the size of a golf ball on the end of my nose.

Oh they had all of the right answers. You had to "grip" the club just so, "stand to the ball" just so, you had to "turn", "bend your knees" just so, "take the club back" just so, have a good "swing thought" (whatever the heck that is, my thought was "knock the hell out of it!"), then you had to "pivot" and drop the club into a "slot" and then BANG!...it was over in an instant. Did it work? No!

Well, I wasn't discouraged. I went to the book store and bought instruction books. I went to the video stores and bought videos up the ying yang. I had a golf library within a month. Oh I had to also subscribe to every golf magazine too. My wife was ready to kill me, and rightly so. It was now an obsession to hit that little white ball.

I flailed at it like a monkey with a hatchet trying to crack a coconut. I looked like one too. Well if I couldn't be a great player I at least had to look good. I watched every tournament every chance I got. I taped tournaments and would stay up until the wee hours of the morning trying to find out that "secret". Hell, there just had to be one. Those guys on TV weren't any bigger than me and made it all look so easy.

I finally relented. I did the unthinkable...I signed up to take golf lessons. Ah, now that just had to work. I was now paying big bucks and just like everything else, you could buy the secret. What could be easier? Oh, why didn't I think of that before? How stupid of me.

I went back to the driving range and met with the instructor. He came highly recommended. He sounded just like the teacher I saw on the videos I had bought...and I had all of them. I knew each one of them by heart. Nothing escaped this attorney's keen eye.

The golf swing was under the microscope and it was going to be conquered like it or not "Mr. Golf Swing". Your butt was mine!

So what happened? I was still flailing away getting nowhere fast. The only thing that was getting better was my teacher's bank account. If it wasn't for putting, I would never have even broken 100. I beat my brains out. I would sneak out of the office early and whack balls until dark night after night. Bang! Bang! Bang!...dribble...boink....clank. I stank.

One Sunday afternoon I went back up to the range and got 3 large buckets of balls. I looked like I should be on tour. I had the clothes, the best clubs, and a fancy staff bag with my name on it. The best golf balls...you name it. Golf was mine.

About half way through the first bucket of embarrassment I noticed that the person behind me was quietly hitting shots. I heard them before I actually looked at where they were going. I was convinced never to look at a crummy player as the bad habits might be contagious. I finally had to see just what was causing this sound of "bullets" coming from behind me.

There was a man in his mid to late 50's in tattered clothes and leather skin wearing a sweat stained visor. He had an old golf bag that had his name on it and the clubs were "blades" which I knew from all of my study were only used by "pros" since they were impossible to hit. He was zipping shot after shot boring into the air. I was sure that he must be cheating some way. No one that I knew, other than the pros I had seen on TV came even close to what this man was doing. The ball bolted off of the clubface and pierced the air leaving a loud stinging sound in its wake. I shook my head. The man looked up for a second and said simply, "Hi." I returned to splaying balls all over the place.

This continued for about another 10 minutes when finally I heard the man from behind me say, "Hey kid." I said, "What?" He said, "You suck." I slowly turned around and said, "Oh, Mr. Holmes I presume?" We both laughed. He said, "Kid, let me show you something." I thought to myself, oh no here we go again. I politely declined but he insisted. He kept pressing me out of pity no doubt. I finally relented.

He asked me, "Kid, you ever heard of a man called Ben Hogan?" I said, "Sure, I have his books and some tapes of him." He said, "Well kid, I was Ben's only student. My name's John, John Schlee." I said, "Nice to meet you. Wow, you know Ben Hogan?" He smiled and said, "Yes. He taught me something many years ago and if you have a minute I'd like to show it to you too. But…"

And this was the big proviso "but". "But kid, you can't tell anyone about this until I'm dead and Mr. Hogan is dead. Promise?" I thought for a nano-second and said, "Hell yes!" He said, "You ever heard of 'The Secret'?" I said, "Sure, everyone has heard of Mr. Hogan's secret." John smiled and said, "Well kid, it ain't in them books you been readin'. Mr. Hogan never put it in the books. He swore me to secrecy and I'm breakin' it. Don't ask me why. I know I'm sick and no one will believe you anyway so here goes."

And away we go... "You wanna know a 'secret'?" Come on in for a minute. That's all it will take.

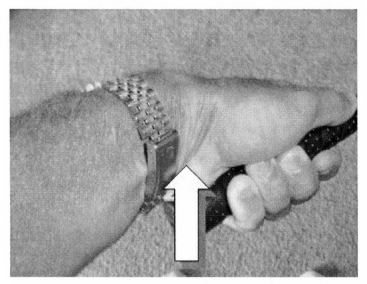

Fig. 1
Left wrist cocked at the 9 o'clock position.
(Note the wrinkles in the wrist)
/\

The "Secret" per John Schlee

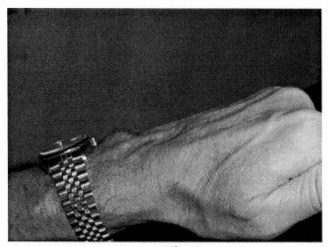

Fig. 2
Left wrist cocked.
(Note the back of the hand is level with the
Forearm and wrist)

13

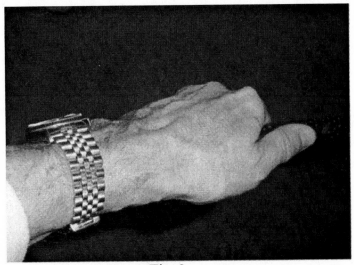

Fig. 3
Left wrist fully uncocked.
(Note the back of the hand is still level with the
Forearm and wrist.)

Fig. 4
Address looking straight down.
(Note no wrinkles in the wrist.)

Discussion

The foregoing photos show "the secret". John told me as follows:

"Kid, you see those wrinkles? (Fig. 1) That's the secret. You hold those as long as you can until you hit the ball. Don't worry about anything but that. If you get to the 9 o'clock position as I'm looking at you, 3 o'clock from your point of view you should have those wrinkles. That's all the wrist cock you can get unless you break your hand off. It won't bend any more than that.

"Now, when I say hold it, I don't mean that you force yourself to hold it like it was welded tight. You don't want anything tight. Nothing. You want that clubhead to be the last thing to get to the ball, not the first thing. Most fellas get the clubhead to the ball first. That doesn't work. Sometimes you'll hit it and other times you won't. Mostly you won't.

Now in reality you can't hold onto the wrist cock since the centrifugal force of the clubhead will undo the wrist cock on its own.

You don't have to think about it. All you need to do is let that clubhead sweep or slide down the plane, I call it trough, and let it...don't force it...let it...hit the ball by itself. The force will pull you up out of the shot into your finish. "Go ahead, try it." John handed me his club

The pros today appear to be "hitting" the ball hard with their hands and arms whereas the claim is that their focus (trust me they are trying to time the impact) is completely on turning toward the target as fast as they can while gently keeping the club on the path to the and through the ball. There is a term that is used "holding the angle". If you try to "hold" the angle you will leave the clubface wide open at impact.

If your hands pass the ball on the downswing before the clubface reaches it you will have to twist the handle to square the face.

The "correction" is to fan the clubface open on the take away and the rotate it shut at impact. (The old "toe up to toe up drill") So with this you have to have not only perfect timing of the body turn, guiding the hands and arms to the point of impact, you now also have the added pressure of getting you clubface rotated into the back of the ball absolutely square.

If you try to correct for these mistakes you must flip your hands to manipulate the clubface squarely into the back of the ball. That takes perfect timing and control which is virtually impossible for a clubhead that is traveling at 80+ miles per hour. Worse if you have 100 + mph.

The amount of centrifugal force generated at that speed is uncontrollable. ANY manipulation will slow the clubhead. Now we come to Newton's Laws there and the law called "Conservation of Angular Momentum".

To elaborate, there are 3 forces at work in the golf swing. First there is the internal force of your body turning back and then through to the target. Anything attached to that internal hub (your body) will turn at a faster speed the further it is away from the center.

The second force comes from the connection of your hands and wrists to the handle. This is the "angle". When the angle is allowed to release behind the turn of the body then there is the creation of angular momentum which was conserved in the wrist cock. As you start your downswing you drop your right elbow down to your right hip keeping the angle created at the top of the backswing. There is no throwing of the clubhead from the top of the backswing. The simultaneous dropping of the right elbow to the hip as you turn your body towards the target loads the shaft as it stays trailing your hands. As your hands reach the ball at the low point in the swing arch the loading on your wrists has reached the maximum tension. Simply let the clubhead fly out away from your body as you continue turning your body towards the target. This loading and snapping effect generate maximum clubhead speed due to the conservation of angular momentum.

If you stood on a turntable holding your arms out to your sides having someone turn you in a circle if you start spinning and you pull your arm into your body you rotation speed increases just as an ice skater does when doing a fast spin on the ice. Essentially, when your hands reach the bottom of the downswing you have in essence pulled your arms in close to your body. If you have played crack the whip on ice with a line of people and the center of the whip stops suddenly the remaining people in the line slow and they hit the tension of the each person up the line. The person on the outside continues on the fastest due to this conservation of angular momentum. Your clubhead is just like the person at the end of the line. The more abrupt the stop at the transition where the hands letting the clubhead snap through the faster it flies.

The final force which deserves only lip service is that of the turning of the clubface it self as it travels on the arc created at the hub. If you even think of trying to control that you are asking for nothing but trouble. The fine tuning of a professional and the years of practice and training can only begin to identify much less master that part of the swing.

If you have ever "chili dipped" a chip shot it was most likely due to your trying to twist the toe of the club quickly through the ball hoping to get the clubface under the ball. That also takes absolute perfect timing. If you don't play all day every day forget that part of the game. Keep your day job.

Another fatal flaw is how you start your swing back to the ball once you've completed your backswing. For those who are inconsistent either slicing horribly or hitting pull-hooks this is the culprit....starting your swing by moving your right shoulder (for right handed players) first.

Once you make the slightest move back to the ball moving your right shoulder first you have killed your chances at hitting a good shot. That tiny move causes you to push the club out over the top thereby forcing the clubhead to the outside of the target path.

For those who have heard the term, "fire your right side" THIS IS NOT THE MOVE.

The proper first move from the top of the backswing is dropping your hands down toward your hip pocket. The clubhead stays behind you on the way down and only starts moving away from you as you toss your hands across your right knee out away from your body while turning your body towards the target.

Your hands are passive and gently holding onto the handle. If you grip it tight, the ball goes right. Tightening your grip slows the clubhead down so when you turn your body the clubhead lags too far behind you and the clubface remains open causing the slice.

The hook happens when you flip your hands and forearms at the last second hoping to square the clubface at impact. YOUR BODY TURN SQUARES THE CLUBFACE

So there are *two motions* that make up your downswing that have to be accomplished smoothly and effortlessly like a dancer not a weight-lifter;

1. Your body turns smoothly towards the target and

2. Your hands and arms as a result of your *natural arm swing,* smoothly swing down and AWAY from your body as it turns the clubhead past the ball. When you slide the clubhead away from the ball you actually rotate your left hand under so as to turn your left palm skyward. This move somewhat shuts the clubface. I know this feels absolutely awkward, and it should, but by doing just that you are setting yourself up for a great golf swing whether is feels like it or not. The snap comes from allowing the clubhead to whip past your hands out and away from your body.

Be sure to SEE the ball hit the clubface!!!!!!

The speed of the clubhead is generated by your body turn, not flipping your hands and forearms. Using your hands to try and square the clubface is like trying to change a tire on a moving car. It causes all sorts of mishaps and if you are having problems making solid contact that is the first place to look. Flipping your hands is fatal.

Essentially, you pull your hands toward you on the back swing and on the down swing you are whipping the clubhead away from your body through the ball up and over your shoulder to a relaxed finish.

Each of us possesses a limit as to just what we can do. Finding that limit comes AFTER you can consistently repeat hitting the ball dead straight.

Your distance is determined by how quickly your body turns towards the target thereby generating speed. Your accuracy is determined by having your clubface square to that target at the moment of impact. The two simple steps above will permit you to hit the ball dead straight.

The distance is a matter of the speed you can comfortably turn your body. Some of us are faster than others.

I recommend that you hit short chip shots so you can feel the coordinated move of your body and arms working together. If the target line is second base from you standing at home plate, then you would turn your body towards second base as you drop the back of your left hand (for right handed players) down toward your hip pocket letting your hands then come close across your right knee swinging out on the line created by your **natural arm swing** which is out towards the second baseman and not the base itself.

Of course the clubhead will not fly out to the second baseman since it is attached to you and it will follow down the target line as your body turns. The clubhead flies up and over your shoulder to a relaxed finish.

Once you understand that the swing is a combination of a smooth body turn towards the target coupled with a tossing of your **natural arm swing** you will be on the road to a repeatable and comfortable golf swing.

What most all amateurs do not understand about professional golfers is just how good that worst guy on tour really is. For the pros "timing is everything".

The great US Open Champion, Johnny Miller, who beat John Schlee for the 1973 US Open, did a clinic for college players after his retirement. He was at the practice range and the lesson went something like this:

"Now you guys are good players. If you weren't, you wouldn't be here or playing for the best golf teams in America. Now you see that flag out there? Let me take this laser and see how far it is. Okay, its 162 to the flag. Now, I am going to take my 162 club here and I have to hit this shot within a yard of that flag."

He nonchalantly hit his 162 club to 2 feet from the flag and got a terrific ovation.

"Now, that wasn't too bad there. Now, without looking or aiming again let me hit another one and see if I can get it as close."

He hit another 162 club shot and the ball landed right next to the one he had hit before. He got a standing ovation. "Now, you guys are at least 3 steps away from being pros. What I mean by that is...I just did that right? Okay, I'm retired. The worst guy out there on tour right now can kick my butt. That's why I don't play anymore."

To say the least the students were in shock. I have had the pleasure of watching several tour professionals doing the exact same thing over and over and over again.

Several years ago I recall taking my neighbor to a "Silly Season" event. He was and is a huge golf fan. I took him out to the practice range where some of the world's leading money winners and legends were warming up. He was in heaven.

I recall us watching one US Open Champion hitting wedge shots of about 100 yards to a practice green. Each shot was landing within a few feet of the pin. My friend was indeed impressed. He whispered to me, "Look at that! I'd kill to be able to do that just once!" I said, "What's the big deal? He missed!" The player heard me and turned around. He smiled and looked at my friend and said, "Sir, he's right. I'm trying to make every one of those, helps my putting stats."

These great players have had the tenacity and talent to learn timing. When the average weekend player starts hitting 600 balls a day 6 or 7 days a week you can probably get some timing and guaranteed some hefty calluses.

That "timing" thing is something you can learn far more quickly once you understand how your swing naturally happens.

First there are some basic principles that govern how a ball flies. These are basics and you will see that a square clubface at impact is all that matters. Once you can master that without manipulation repeatedly then you can make minor adjustments deliberately to affect the ball's flight. The basic balls rotation comes from the direction and angle at which the clubface collides with the ball. See the following illustrations on the following pages.

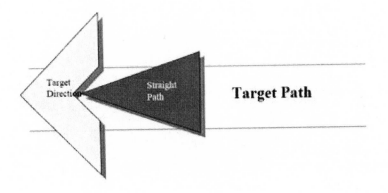

Fig. 5
PATH & Ball Flight
Target Path
Target
Direction
(Theoretic) Straight
Path

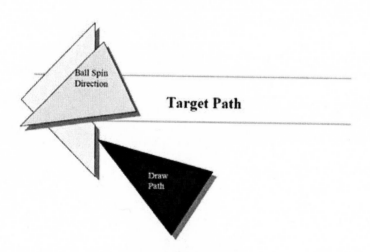

Lower Trajectory
Fig. 6
Target Path
Lower Trajectory
Ball Spin
Direction
Draw
Path

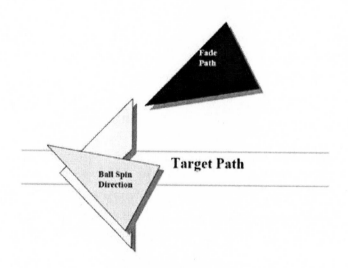

Higher Trajectory
Fig. 7
Target Path
Higher Trajectory
Ball Spin
Direction
Fade
Path

You use no more manipulation or physical force in your hands and arms than you would employ using a spoon or a fork when you eat. The less tension you have in your hands and arms the faster your body can move them past the ball. John Schlee never used the word "hit".

"Kid, there is no pulling of the club handle to the ball. Just let the clubhead find its way to the back of the ball as you turn your body. As you get used to sweeping the ball off of the tee straight, and I don't care how far right now...THEN you can gently and slowly start to increase the speed you use to turn your body past the ball as the clubhead follows you through to the finish. Think of the club coming through last, never first.

Remember this if you don't remember anything else today... YOU CAN'T CONTROL THE CLUB HEAD ANYWAY NO MATTER HOW HARD YOU TRY. YOU CAN ONLY SLIGHTLY ALTER THE PATH IT TAKES TO THE BALL AND THAT STARTS RIGHT FROM THE TOP."

Well that one I took to heart. If I thought of anything from then on it was turning my left shoulder over my right foot (I'm right-handed) and then simply turning to face the target. Now that sounds too easy. It is.

Fig. 8

Left Wrist at Address

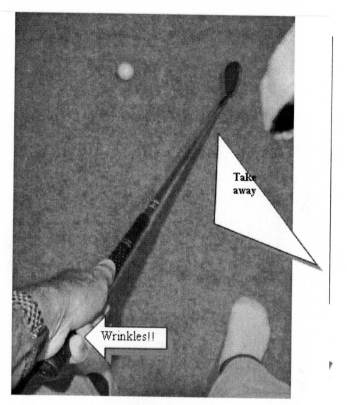

Fig. 9

First move back

This angle is looking straight down, player's POV.

The left hand is moving in the same direction as the clubface not toward the target.

(Supination delofts the club and closes the face)

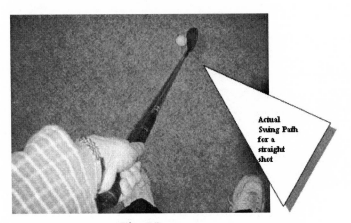

Fig. 10

Left Wrist Supinated simulated at impact

The left hand is moving in the same direction as the clubface not toward the target.

(Supination delofts the club and closes the face)

KEEP THE CLUB FACE SQUARE TO TARGET PATH
AS LONG AS POSSIBLE ON TAKE AWAY AND ON
THE RETURN TO THE BALL

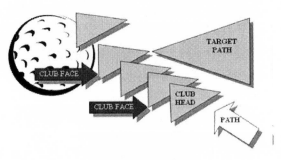

FANNING THE CLUB FACE
OPEN OR CLOSED
IS FATAL

Fig. 11

"The" Secret

The reality of the swing is that the clubface comes into the ball at an "inside path" due to the ***natural arm swing***. When you walk notice how your arms swing. Don't force the movement just be aware of the motion. Your arms swing toward an imaginary intersecting point somewhere directly in front of your body and not in a line the runs parallel to your path.

Imagine you are walking down the center of a railroad track. There is a track on either side of you. Your arms do not swing along the path of the tracks but at an angle that intersects with the center of your path between the two tracks. This natural arm swing is the natural path that your clubhead must be following in order to achieve the proper swing plane. This is just how a human body naturally moves.

If you manipulate the movements then in order to repeat that manipulation you have to, at some level, think about performing the movement. In a natural motion it just happens. *The "Secret"* is NOT the wrinkles but IS the **_natural arm swing_**. As you draw the club away from the ball you try to rotate your body and keep the clubface square to the target line as possible. Let your right elbow break naturally. Don't yank the club straight back. It will follow your body as it turns. Let the club go up gently and smoothly. You'll find that your weight is not directly over your right foot (right-handers) as it should be. You stop your back swing when your body tells you that you have gone far enough. Don't force it. You'll just knock yourself off balance.

To start the downswing think as if you were now going to naturally left your right hand return to its natural position as it would be hanging from your arm as letting it move in front of you carrying you around as it you were taking a ping pong paddle and attempting to slap the ball with a little top spin on it.

Actually your clubface will return to the ball squarely from this natural motion at the critical moment of impact. The back of your right hand should be pointing towards the sky as you reach the ¾ way through your swing and ultimately the momentum will turn your body so it faces the target with the club now comfortably over your left shoulder.

All of this is done in a relaxed fashion. You can start with a wedge and toss little chips to a target. I tend to think of holding a knife in my right hand and making a stabbing motion with it following the natural motion of my ***natural arm swing.***

Let your right hand hang at your side and curl your fingers up into your palm. Let your thumb stick out as if you were getting ready to hitch hike. Now let your arm start swing as you would if you were walking letting your body swing with it. As you increase the length of hand swinging finally allow it to go back with your body turning naturally with it and then let your right hand swing that thumb up and over your left shoulder allowing your body to flow right along with it. Do not force the swinging motion. Just let it happen. Do it several times increasing the speed each time you do it. You will find that you can do it rapidly and keep your balance at the same time. Let your body turn in unison with this arm swing. It is your BODY TURN that squares your clubface at impact not your hands and forearms. Your arms swing out and away from your body as you are simultaneously turning toward the target. The target line, as illustrated above is a function of your body.

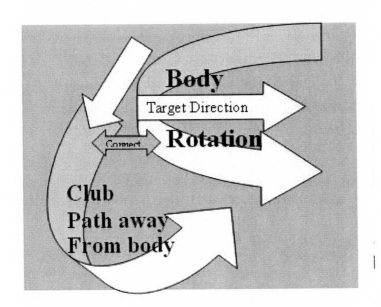

Rotation Paths

Fig. 12

Now, take a regular old screw driver out and start swinging underhand over your shoulder. Feel the rhythm as you do. DO NOT FORCE IT. LET it happen. As you get used to this new natural motion you can move to using a sand wedge letting the club slide back and forth. Add your left hand to the handle and rock the club back and forth.

Once you feel a bit more comfortable, chip a ball to a target like a coaster. You need to develop the feel that you are TOSSING the ball to the little target. It will take some getting used to. But with practice you'll no longer be hoping for a big wide fairway. You'll be hoping for that bowling alley and hitting the target dead on!

Ball Spin

The left or right spin you put on the ball comes from the rotation of the forearms and hands. For a right handed player an abrupt counter-clockwise turn at impact puts the counter-clockwise (draw) spin on the ball. Holding the clubface "open" puts the clockwise (fade) on the ball. One should be mindful that when you are using the ***natural arm swing*** approach into the ball that the leading edge of the club will determine the initial direction of the ball and the motion of the clubface surface as it slides across the ball determines the spin.

If on your take away you rotate your forearms you will have to rotate them an equal amount at impact. The clubhead is moving far too quickly to make the precision adjustments like those and therefore only the most skillful and naturally gifted can repeat such movements with predictable regularity.

Take a flat faced screw driver and try to place it the slot on the head of a screw as you swing it by at 80 mph! But, you CAN jab that screw driver into a melon sitting on a stool with great speed and efficiency without twisting your wrist.

With the ***natural arm swing***, without manipulation, you can hit the ball predictably. You can hit it to a predictable point and connect the dots around the course. Distance is what is natural for you. Knowing what you can do at any given point permits you to avoid the hazards in your way and "your best level" of play. You can repeatedly return the clubface squarely to the back of the ball each time you swing your arms without any manipulation. The sensation of the back of your left hand (right handed players) dropping into the back of the ball is what you want to feel.

Drill

Without a club, take your relaxed address position. Let your arms and wrists just hang loosely.

Turn your body completely away from the target. Do this comfortably...NOT strained in any fashion. Your back should be facing the target and you should be facing in the opposite direction. Your arms are limp. Most of your weight should be on your right foot. (step to the right)

While facing away from the target, stretch your arms away (not across) from your body. Raise your arms up to the level of your right shoulder. The back of your left hand should be parallel to the target line at the top as you are still facing away from the target. That is the extension you want at the top of your backswing. Your right elbow is NOT touching your side.

Leaving your arms comfortably extended, drop the back of your left hand back towards your right foot slowly letting your wrists stay limp.

As your hands reach your waist turn your body back to the target swinging your arms away from you up and over your left shoulder as you allow your left wrist naturally flip (or release) from the conservation of angular momentum to a balanced finish.

Your weight should be on your left foot and you should be up on your right toe facing the target.

It is the extension combined with one smooth motion from the top to the finish that you want to achieve. There is no deliberate acceleration (or hit) at the bottom of the swing. The entire motion should feel smooth and relaxed with no tension.

The more relaxed you perform the motion the easier it is to allow the centrifugal force keep you on plane. It is more of a smooth dance motion as opposed to a forceful hit that you would use to pound a nail.

Enlightenment

There are all sorts of theories out there and they are all different and many times contradict one another. Perhaps Mr. Hogan was wrong. What have you got to lose but a few strokes off of your score card? You watch the world's finest players each week and you can see that they don't hit every fairway, every green or even make every putt. You can't expect to do any better than that. If you were that bad you wouldn't be reading this booklet. You would be out in California at Q-school getting your PGA Tour card

You must always keep in mind that golf is a "target" game. Distance is useless without accuracy. Oh sure it is great to see the pros hit the ball a country mile. And it is thrilling to see a major league ballplayer knock one out clear out of the park. But, even the greatest hitters in the game hit foul balls or even strike out from time to time.

It is totally unrealistic for a weekend warrior to think that he or she can even come close to what the TV millionaires can do.

There is a story about kid and his first lesson with teacher down in Texas. The kid was about 7 and his dad had had some clubs cut down to size and wanted him to learn the game.

The teacher took little fellow out to the practice tee and he had him tee up a ball. He told the boy to take dead aim at a flag stick about 75 yards away. The kid did and hit is sawed-off 7 iron within a few feet of the pin on the first try.

The teacher was elated and said, "Come on son, take your putter and we'll go out there and you can knock the ball into the hole." The youngster looked at his teacher with a confused look on his face and shook his little head and said, "Why didn't you say you wanted me to knock it in the hole? Now we have to walk!"

Needless to say, the teacher was impressed that the boy knew that hitting the target was all that mattered.

When you think about it, does it really matter if you took 4 shots, 150 yards each, to reach that par 5, you'd be out 600 yards! Hit 3, 150 yard shots and you're now out 450 yards from the tee which is a really long par 4 on most courses.

Now if you know you can predictably hit a ball 150 yards into a 15' X 15' square, you're on to something. A 15' putt for par!

Or is it more important for you to hit your drive 260 yards behind a tree, hit the tree with your next shot knocking your back 20 yards right next to a bush where you have to use a "Foot wedge" to kick the ball out so you can hit it, (Oh, be sure no one sees you do it), then, completely frazzled, "top" your next shot for about 50 yards into the right rough where the ball "needs" a little education as to just how it should lie, then "slice" a

5 iron into the front bunker leaving you a good 3 or 4 strokes (you take 2) and finally hit it 10 yards over the green, then you chip it back 30 feet past the hole and3 putt your way to the score card where you "honestly" put down 7?

The point here is that all you are going to remember is that you hit the ball 260 yards off the tee! Somehow the logic makes no sense. And of course, none of us has ever done that before.

Many of the world's great players learn that physics rules how a person moves about this world no matter what we think we do. Each step you take is dependent on the Earth's gravity holding you down. The fatter you are the harder the Earth pulls you down on the scale.

There are volumes written on the grip and stance. My feeling is if you feel the least bit strained in any part of your setup something is amiss. You should always feel alert but relaxed. Your attention should be directed to keeping a light grip pressure. On a scale of 1 to 10 with 10 being the tightest, I would recommend nothing stronger than a 3. Tight muscles cannot move freely and they restrict your motion necessary to generate clubhead speed. It is the snap like you would use to striking a match that you are trying to achieve. Brute force is fine for lifting weights but has no business in a smooth free golf swing.

"Supination" of the left hand and wrist at impact is an important factor. [See Fig 10] The left wrist would actually bow out toward the target. This "supination" is the result of letting the clubhead remain last in the swing. There is no deliberate pressing or shoving of the left wrist at the target. Quite the contrary, if anything the clubhead was being gently dragged into the bag of the ball and the wrist simply bent letting the clubhead linger for a only a split second before impact.

This "supination" results in this "de-lofting" of the clubface. This amounts to a relaxation of the left wrist.

The mystery of the cupped left wrist

The "cupped left wrist" at the top of the swing which Mr. Hogan had in his swing was really not a "secret" but more of a trick to throw his competitors off track. After dissecting his swing frame by frame I found an amazing thing. He did cup his wrist at the top. I struggled trying to figure out just how he managed to have his wrist in the opposite position at impact. It seemed almost impossible. If you recall earlier I mention the rolling of the left wrist under (Pronating). As he dropped his arms back to his side he rolled that cupping out to the Supinated position at the beginning of his downswing which actually gave him added extension and a bit more clubhead speed without any added effort. It wasn't until I tried it myself that I was convinced it worked and low and behold it did immediately.

I truly believe that Mr. Hogan cupped his left wrist to fool his competitors into believing he was using the old school Scottish Pronating method. He obviously wasn't. I am sure that this has led to all of the speculation as to just what he was up to and the mystery of his "secret". Whether it is a secret or not is of no consequence. This simple but effective method works!! And it works well!

I would not recommend adding this little move to your swing until you feel extremely comfortable using the methods outlined above. It will not work until you master these easy steps. But once you do, get ready for some real excitement!

Also, as the saying goes, "A good man knows his limitations." If you are 55 years old and been hacking balls around the local muni for years, you're 5' 8" tall and weigh 195 lbs. you can't expect to play like a tiger who is less than half your age, in perfect physical shape, does nothing but play golf and smile.

Even best players miss a shot now and then. The key for all "smart" players...is knowing how to avoid more trouble. All great players never play a shot they haven't practiced to death.

Never expect a miracle. Sure everyone gets lucky now and then but...somehow the harder you practice and the more you hone your skills the luckier you get. Funny how that works. There is no such thing as an "Over-night success." All of the world's best at anything got there through hard work and planning. Some of us are born with better attributes for different things. Some are great golfers. Some are great mothers. Some are great scientists. What ever the discipline, everyone who is any good at it had a propensity for the skill and excelled at it. There are very few Mozart's out there. We all wish we could be one. If you're not, then you just have to learn to accept that and move on.

The USGA developed the handicapping system so that we could all compete with one another on a level playing field. There is no dishonor in hitting from the tees set up for those of us that aren't tour players. "Getting your money's worth" and "Seeing all of the course" are sorry reasons for high scores when the rules have already been bent in your favor. You are only cheating yourself and others out of you playing the best "you" can play.

There is no harm for a short person to use a ladder to see the parade. That is fair and no one can fault the small person that aid. Use everything there is to your advantage. You can use the rules to beat guys half your age, and beat them soundly. The handicap system levels the playing field and there is no reason that you can't "cheat" when the rules make it perfectly acceptable to do just that.

When you think of it, we divide up marathon running by age group. A 60 year old can't expect to beat a 19 year old Olympic Gold Medal winner. But, the 60 year old sure as hell can beat the other 60 year olds, if he gives it his best shot. There is the lesson we teach our children, "DO YOUR BEST." Whatever that "YOUR" is, do it.

One story I heard from that famous little Puerto Rican golfer, Chi Chi Rodriguez, more years ago than I care to admit, was how being "SSSSLLLLOOOOWWWW" was so important. He told me once, "When I have to play golf in the morning, I wake up slow, I go to the bathroom slow, I take my shower slow, I get dressed slow, I eat my breakfast slow, I walk to the car slow, I drive to the golf course slow, I walk to the locker room slow, I practice slow, I hit the ball slow, I putt some slow, I walk to the first tee slow, I tee up the ball and swing slow, I play the whole tournament slow.....and..... When I go to the bank....I RUN!"

There is no sense trying to kill the ball. After all what did that little ball ever do for you. Take a mid-iron and swing as described above trying to clip the top of the grass. Gradually increase the clubhead speed to make a cleaner cut. Try in cut a path clipping away. You will feel there is no real muscular effort needed to generate a lot of clubhead speed to clip the grass. There golf swing is nothing more than using this clipping motion letting the ball get in the way. As you clip the grass you will hear a "swoosh" and the faster you swing the louder the "swoosh" thus the faster the clubhead and the truer the arch.

Once you learn to "swoosh" the ball you will hit it straighter...maybe not "longer"...but always remember to say to yourself, "What in the hell is wrong with being in the fairway?" Sure Barney might be out there 50 yards past you behind a tree. But all the extra "distance" gets Barney is being left holding the check at the 19th hole. You can take great pride in being the "little Ben" (both of them) and beat the pants off anyone at your club just by being "you". What's wrong with that? I put it to you...what in the world is wrong with that?

Start practicing chipping and not making full swings to start. I usually begin with a pitching wedge. I take my setup comfortably and focus on hitting my shots straight. I am right handed so my description here is from my point of view. I set the clubface behind the ball with its leading edge perpendicular to the intended target. My move away from the ball is left hand gently rolling under or supinating combined with my stepping my weight over to my right foot as if I was walking. My body and shoulders turn in unison with the club. I take it back far enough to hit about 15 feet. Once I have completed the backswing I simply step back to my left foot ALLOWING the back of my left hand to drop back down towards the ball as my chest turns back to the target. AS A RESULT the clubhead drops into the back of the ball as it swing AWAY from my body. My body squares the clubface.]

There is a definite sense of rhythm and timing. My knees feel as if they are more springy than rigid. My hands and forearms are passive at all times. I have the sensation of almost dragging the clubhead as it drops into the ball. The ball literally pops off the clubhead as the clubhead falls down and through as my chest turns to the target.

The full swing is really nothing more than a longer version of this chip. The longer the swing back and through, the further the ball flies. Practice taking the clubhead a bit farther back with each swing duplicating the path stepping to the right and then smoothly back to the left.

If you are willing to devote your life to hitting it close and making every putt then you are going to have to quit your day job. If not, then just go out and enjoy the fresh air and your buddies. There is nothing wrong with that. You may never be a professional tour player. But, you have one thing going for you now...You know "The" Secret.   Throw a thumb over your shoulder.

THE SECRET
TO A GREAT GOLF SWING

The Mike Cortson Company
SHSSH! LLC
© 2006